Garden of Verses

Volume 2

ELLA RITA UQUAK

ISBN: 978-1-960764-61-4 (sc)
ISBN: 978-1-960764-62-1 (hc)

Write and Release
PUBLISHING

www.writeandreleasepublishing.com

ACKNOWLEDGEMENT

To Him, who started it all, and saw me through every winding
path, to the finishing line, I give Him all the glory.
In the enchanting notes of the bloomy,"Garden Of Verses"
and the flourishing rhythms of joy, God is exalted.

Walking through the tunes of time, they lit my path with lingering fragrance
of love, and bountiful notes of joy, showering me with rides of affection, my
parents, Prof Isaac Solomon Dema, and Joan Dema, of blessed memories.
Thanks for all the love.

To my wonder man, delightful, and energetic, passionate, and success
driven, my love, my hubby, who supported, and encouraged me
tremendously, and has been greatly excited to see this venture come to
fruition, as it makes its way to the pages of reality, my Special Thanks....

To my treasured, adorable, cherished, and loving children,
Charles Jr, and Joshua, who showed admiration for the work,
while in process, and gave words of encouragement, which
boosted me, I appreciate your love, and support.

In their own special, and beautiful way, my loving brothers who have greatly
touched my life, with many interesting, memorable moments, and expressed
joy, on getting this book out. Denis gave words of encouragement, and
expressed delight on the project, Akenobi, greatly encouraged and inspired
me to get the work out, Perisuo showed sweet sentiments, as he voiced
out congratulations, on the project. My brothers, my joy, and to Idiami
for all the fun times, we shared while, he walked the isles of mortality.

Sweetly, and preciously, with such vibrance and warmth, they
have added zest to my life, my lovely, adorable, sisters-in-law
Bernice, Lizzy, Pat, and Sarah, I appreciate you all.

To a very special lady, who has walked many miles with me,
stood by me, and showered me with unwavering love, Mrs
Iminabo Opuoyibo, my friend, my sister, you are amazing.

Table of Contents

A Dreamy World

Roses in splendor,
Rose Quartz in petals,
Pink Morganite in
rosey blooms!
It's the twinkles, and
jingles of roses,
that makes it;
"A Dreamy World!"

A New Glow

A new glow of,
Joy! Peace! Love!
Swirls around me!

Astonishing Wonder

In astonishing
wonder!
May you be
wrapped in
His goodness!

Beaming Moon

On a cold night,
I see the moon,
like a dazzling
piece of silver,
up the night sky;
Its soft beam, brings
feelings of exhilaration!
It lights the lonely sky, with a
gleam of hope!
God is exalted!
He made the "Great Lights"
He made all things, great and small;
God is exalted!
Let the moon glow,
and give light to the earth.
God is exalted!

Beautiful Experience

The beautiful things of
nature, keeps us smiling;
The strength of His love,
keeps us hopeful.

Beauty In Barn

There is beauty in my barn,
The petal clap of roses,
The festal joy of rising blooms!
Love is rekindled! Hope is reborn!

Blinking Love

Let me play with you,
Let me sing with you,
Let me dance with you,
Let me feel your warmth,
Let me drink from you,
Let me taste your nectar,
For when the sun sets,
I will be gone.

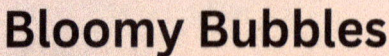

Bloomy Bubbles

As a flower blossoms in glowy
radiance of love!
May you daily blossom in the
glow of His grace!
May His brightness bring you
joy!
May your dreams come true on
the ride of cherry blossoms!
May your hopes blossom on
fresh notes of a new day!
May the songs of dawn uplift
you!
May sweet whispers of bloomy
joy be yours always,
May you blossom sweetly in
glowy radiance of love!
May favour come blooming
your way!

Blooms Of Radiance

Blooms of elegance, and joy!
Royalties of the garden!
Luxuriant and radiant in red,
Blooms of delight, springing
forth in beauty;
Charming and singing out
rhythms of love and joy;
Precious roses, blooming
out in splendor!

Bloomy Awake

Turn new pages open!
Beauty is reborn!
The daisies bloom again!
Hope sings a floral song!

Bloomy Love

Let love flourish,
as the blooms;
Let joy be lit your
way, as its crispy
scent, lights the
garden.

Bloomy Spring

In glowing fields, we
spring up again!
In glowing fields, we
sing a new song,
In glowing mercies of
each new day,
May the Lord, shine His
love on you.

Blossom In Radiance

A merry joyful glow!
A merry joyful ring of
radiant blooms, at the
dial of dawn!
Merry-n-Glowy, rise to a
beautiful bloomy day!

Charming Glow

Delectable in floral reticence she glows in charming wonder!
She adorns the garden in pearlescent beauty,
Dressed in costly rainments, colours of alluring beauty!
Could it be you?
Could it be me?
Could it be the glow of a sweet Summer night?
Could it be the rhythmical glow that brightens the sky?
Could it be the bloomy pearls singing in a love lit garden?
Could it be the precious gems glazing the garden in love?
Could be the dancing trail of stars that loom the night sky!
Could be the sparkly bubbles of the singing galaxies!
Could be the dazzling glow of love lit in a million pebbles!
Could be the garden Queen glowing in bloomy radiance!
In all beauty and grandeur a charming wonder to behold!

Colourful Song

Love is a colourful song,
with enlivening notes!

Comforting Voice

"When all goes quiet, love still speaks; with a voice that, comforts the heart."

Corridors Of Joy

May you walk,
in the corridors
of joy!
May you walk,
in the strength
of His love!

Creation Sings

Your greatness is told at the,
mountain top!
Your majesty is sang in the,
clouds!
Creation rings out your praise, O Lord!

Crispy Love

A joyful play of
petals!
Crispy droplets,
of love;
Joy in wonder!
An expression,
of love!

Crystal Love Drop

It's a crystal drop of joy!
An awake to bloomy dawn,
A drip of dewy crystals!
It's a crystal love drop,
A sparkle of favor on the,
soft dainty blooms.

Daisy Glow

"Sweet Daisy Radiance"
Dainty and Glamorous,
Frilly corals in bloom!
Flamboyant-n-Glowy!
A sweet touch of joy!
A radiant touch of love!
In beauty you touch,
hearts with joy!

Dawn Joy

May beauty find you,
at the wake of dawn,
When the sun bells,
chime the rhythms
of a new day, may
favor be yours;
May joy be yours,
always!

Delightful Fields

May the Lord, take
you to pleasurable
fields bursting with
enchanting notes!
May the sweet
floral fragrance,
refresh you.

Divine Presence

May the beauty of the Lord,
surround you on every shore.

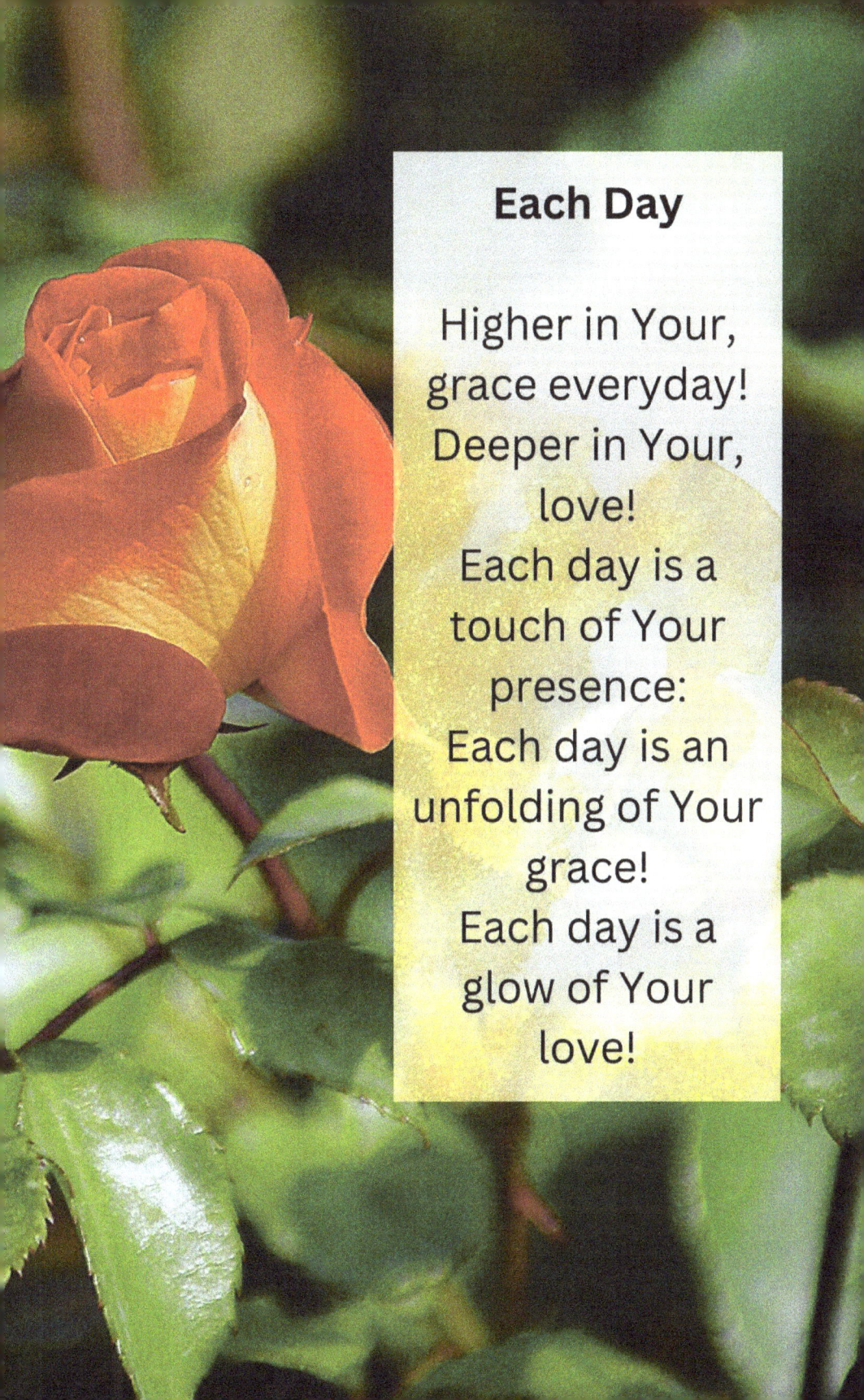

Each Day

Higher in Your, grace everyday!
Deeper in Your, love!
Each day is a touch of Your presence:
Each day is an unfolding of Your grace!
Each day is a glow of Your love!

Elegant Bloom

In glowing
beauty!
She adorns
the garden,
She stuns
in elegance,
She is a
radiance,
of hope.

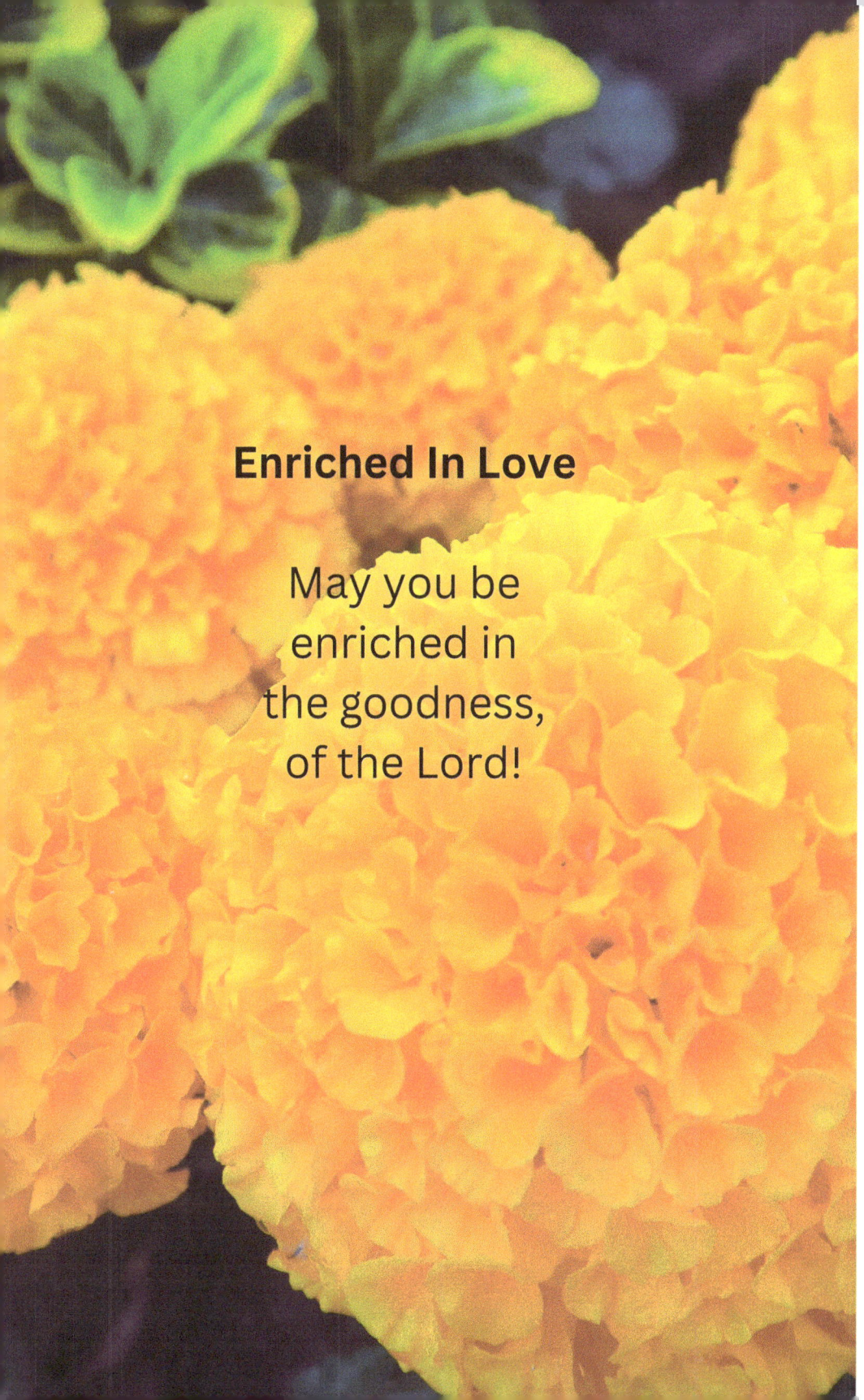

Enriched In Love

May you be
enriched in
the goodness,
of the Lord!

Fall Delight

Russet brown metamorphosing sweetly to luscious red
Curls of leafy greens embracing shades of fruity olive green
Vibrant notes of berry red leaves kissing the captivating sunset
Golden bronze leaves dancing joyfully to breezy tones
It's a joyful Fall delight! Colours of Fall in glow!
A swing to the rhythms and tunes of Fall!
A touch of mustard yellow splashes on leaves
A swirl of orange tones cascading the season
A bounce of nutty browns unfolding graciously
Vivid hues of gold, red, yellow, orange, and brown, lit in
decorative leafy carpets of beauty!
It's all a Fall wonder! A majestic nod of Fall.

Fancy Glow

In sweet touches of Red Beryl
gemstones, on lacy and delicate
petals of luxurious blooms,
Moussaieff Red Diamonds come
a-glow!
Like the Red Beryl gemstones in
rosey-glowy-blooms!
Like the fancy glow of Moussaieff
Red Diamonds!
Love glows fancifully in the heart
of roses!
Love blooms preciously as roses!

Floral Aisles

May you walk on
floral aisles; filled
with the sounding
notes of joy!
May florals chant
love your way!

Floral And Sweet

Sweet floral notes!
A touch of joy in pink!
A touch of love in red!
A touch of sparkling
floral elation;
A touch of His love!

Floral Bliss

It's a song of return, a sweet note!
Echoes of floral joy resounds!
It's the bountiful return of florals, In
beauty they reminiscence the
sweetness of life;
I love to watch them dance to the
soft tunes of the Spring breeze;
In joy they sing their sweet return.

Floral Gem

Like a star in the
fields!
She glitters,
adorned with
sweet droplets
She is "Salsify."

Floral Hearts

Floral hearts
unveiled at dawn;
"Love, Joy, Beauty,"
play a tune in
those hearts.

Floral Lightning

In a world lit by
florals!
Let love blossom,
Let peace flourish,
in every home.

Floral Rhythms

Filling the moments with beauty,
Enveloping the garden in joy,
Embracing the season with love!
The scent of "Lady Rose."

Floral Whispers

Love blooms
as a fancy glow!
It sings with
floral notes,
It whispers in
the wind, on
the ride of
floral scents!
Love is a
precious song,
energizing, and
uplifting.

Floral Wishes

Wishing you a sweet bloomy, bountiful, flow of positivity; May the sweet scent of floral bliss envelop you!

Flowing Streams

As flowing
streams,
May joy,
flow
your way
always.

Floxy Radiance

May the sweet notes of florals,
bring you whispers of joy,
hope, peace, and love.

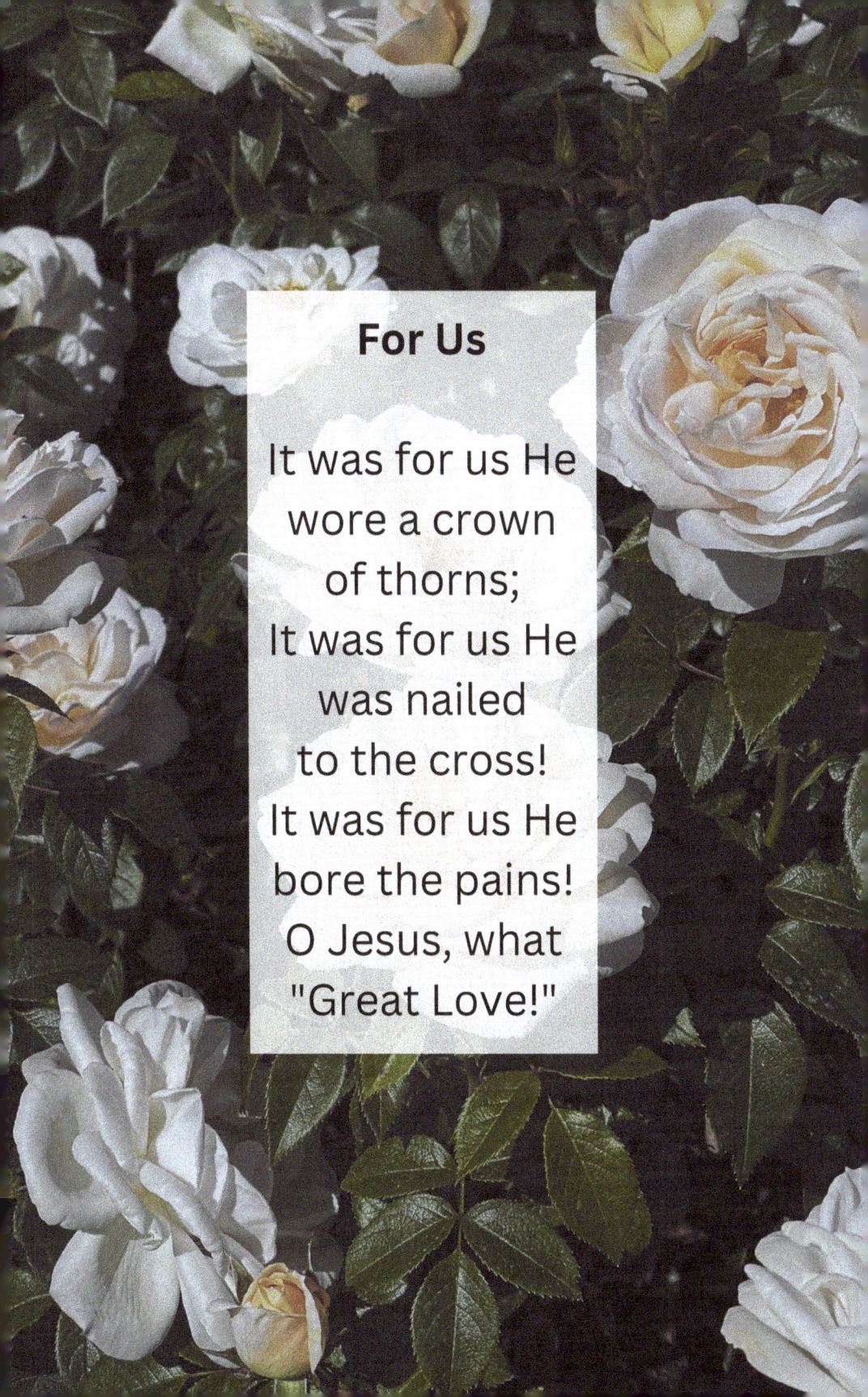

For Us

It was for us He
wore a crown
of thorns;
It was for us He
was nailed
to the cross!
It was for us He
bore the pains!
O Jesus, what
"Great Love!"

Fresh Petals

On fresh petals,
I sing to you!
May you be,
"Laced by Love"
"Spiced by Love"
"Coated by Love"

Fragrance On A Ride

Fragrance on a ride, candied
dewy blooms at dawn!
Fragrance on a ride, sweet
essence of enchanting blooms!
Fragrance on a ride, the blushing
notes of floral joy!
Merry tunes of whispering
flowers cascading on fragrant
notes, Fragrance on a ride,
warms our hearts with joy!
Fragrance on a ride, the
whimsical dance of bouncy
flourishing blooms!
Love blissfully lights the air with
fragrance on a ride!

From Coast To Coast

From coast to coast
Your greatness is
chanted!
From coast to coast
You are magnified!
From coast to coast
You reign O LORD!
From coast to coast
You are glorified;
From coast to coast
There is none like
You!
Yes LORD from coast
to coast!

Gentle Touch

May the beauty
of love be yours!
May the radiance
of joy always add
sparkles to your day.

Glaze Of Joy

As the dew
glazes the grass
with sparkling
droplets!
May His love
be glazed over
you in sparkling
wonder!

Glowing Song

Could I ever say goodbye...
Could I ever say the glow is gone....
Could I ever say the flowers have faded....
Could I ever say the sparrows sing no
more...
For even when the curtains are drawn...
"Love still glows!"
For even when night time creeps in....
"Your song is still heard"
For even when all is silent...
"Your voice still echoes in the wind"
Could I ever say goodbye..
For the colours of love never fades!

Glow Of Comfort

In the strength of His love
may you find comfort
everyday;
In the glow of His grace
may you flourish
in bountiful joy.

Glow Of Love

With the glow
of His love;
With the joy
of His mercy.

May you be
renewed in
His presence
everyday.

Glow Of Renewal

Flashes of love!
Glow of renewal,
May you be,
refreshed everyday.

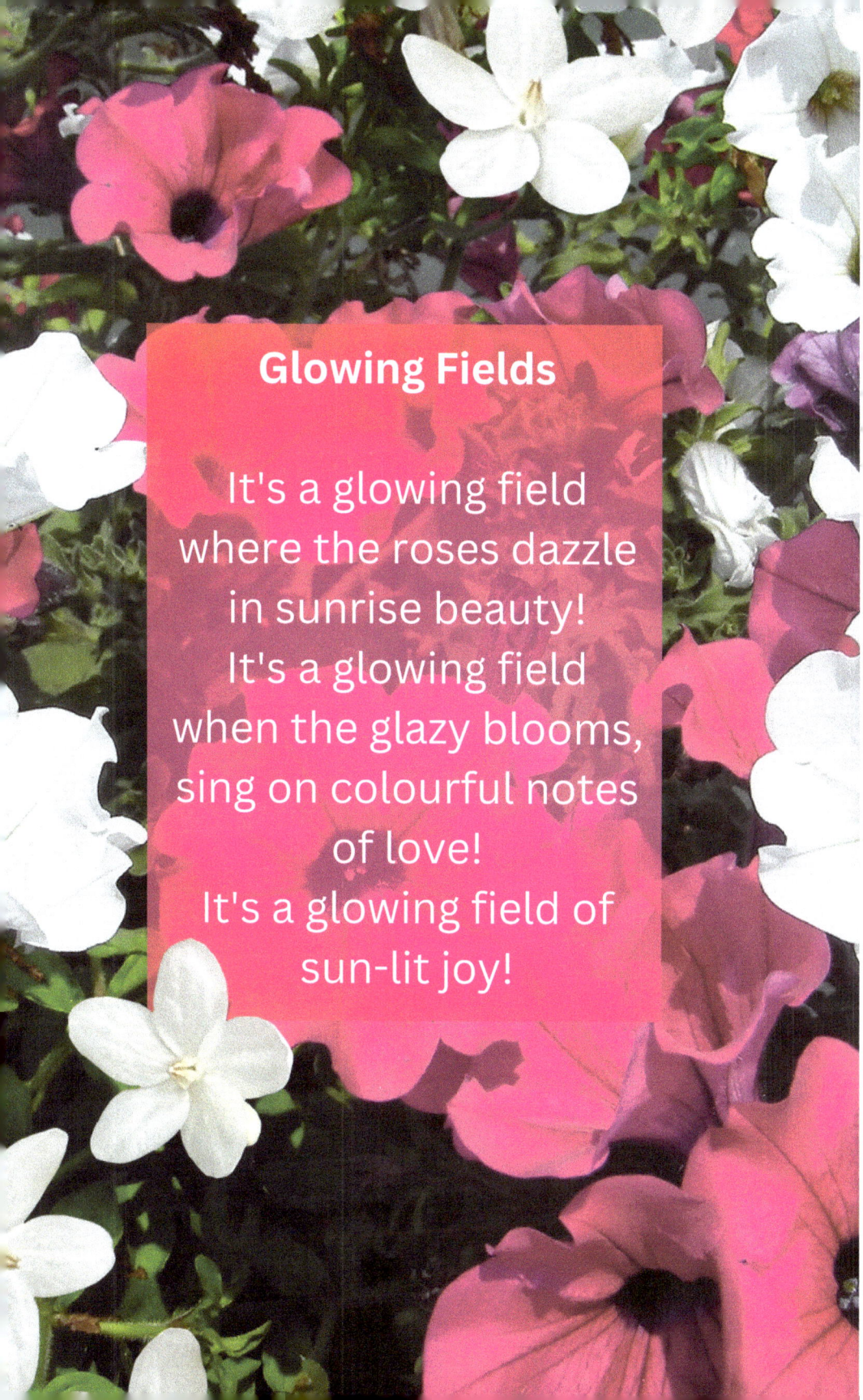

Glowing Fields

It's a glowing field
where the roses dazzle
in sunrise beauty!
It's a glowing field
when the glazy blooms,
sing on colourful notes
of love!
It's a glowing field of
sun-lit joy!

Glowing Through

Even in the
darkest night,
love finds its
way, and glows
through the,
darkest tunnel.

Golden Gift

True friendship, is like pure gold!
It stands the test of time,
Attesting its worth, and
value.

Golden Moments

Every chance to light up a smile, is a golden
moment,
Treasure it!
Every chance to walk the dew-kissed grass, is
a golden moment,
Treasure it!
Every chance to pick up gorgeous blooms, is a
golden moment,
Treasure it!
Treasure the moments that wraps you in
flowery cuddles!
Treasure the moments that kindles the
rainbow in the sky!
Treasure the moments that lights peace in
the air!
Treasure the moments that walks you
through the glazy paths,
"Of Joy"
Treasure the golden lit moments of love!

Golden Touch

Touch me with the,
colours of your love!
Wrap me in shawls,
of your glow;
Take me to fields,
where beauty,
blooms like flowers.

Highest Expression

He is the Highest,
expression of
"Love,"

He is the Deepest,
expression of
"Grace,"

He is Jesus.

His Mercies

In splashes and
in dips
In joy and wonder
His goodness is
written all over us!
His mercies are
written all over us!
His love is written
all over us!
We are children
of God.

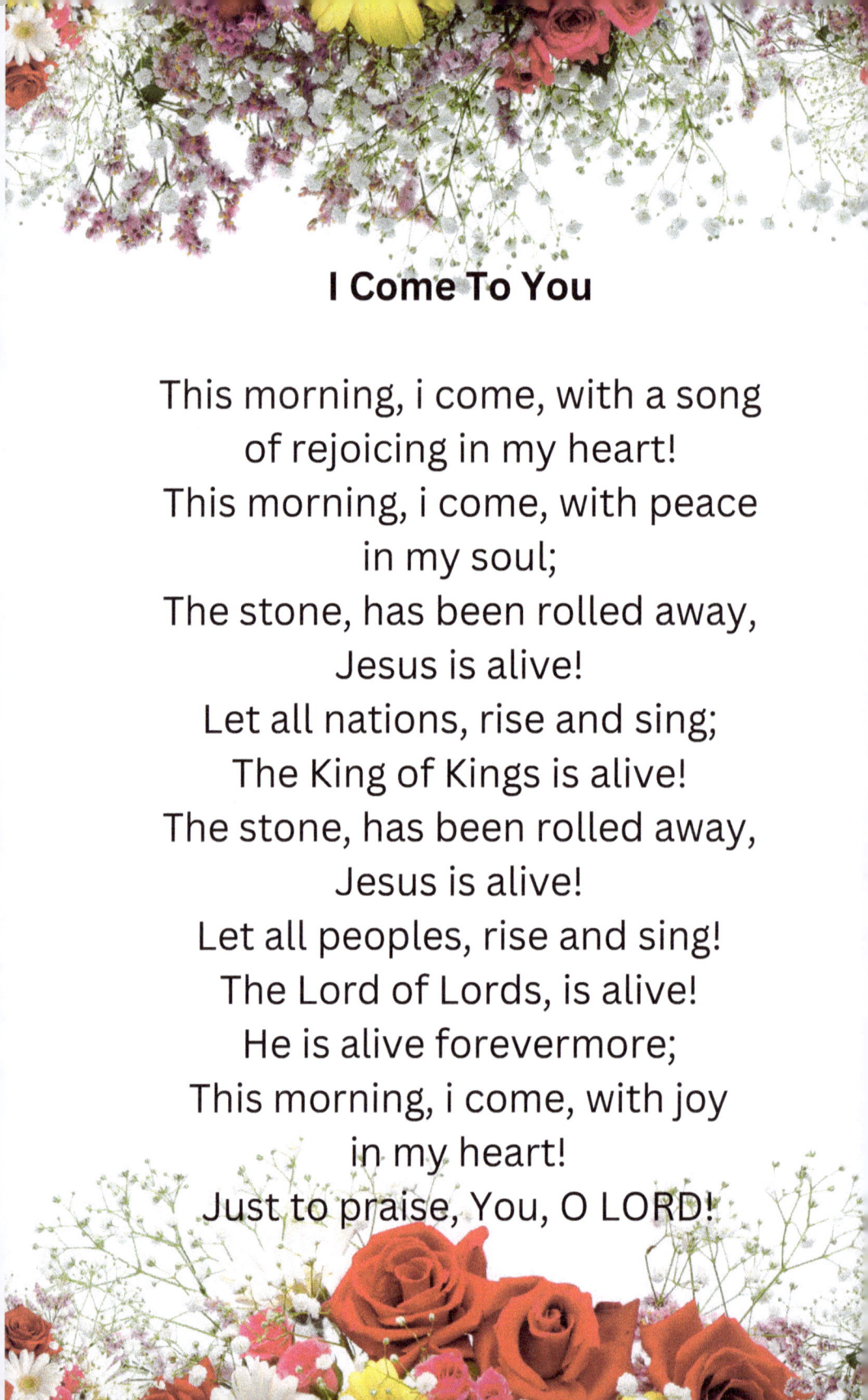

I Come To You

This morning, i come, with a song
of rejoicing in my heart!
This morning, i come, with peace
in my soul;
The stone, has been rolled away,
Jesus is alive!
Let all nations, rise and sing;
The King of Kings is alive!
The stone, has been rolled away,
Jesus is alive!
Let all peoples, rise and sing!
The Lord of Lords, is alive!
He is alive forevermore;
This morning, i come, with joy
in my heart!
Just to praise, You, O LORD!

In Hope

As a flower opens up its petals,
to receive warmth from the sun;
so I open up my hands, to receive
blessings from you O Lord!

In Glowing Love

Fill me in the morning, with your glow
and love!
Touch me in the evening, with your
tender mercies;
Your love O Lord, is everlasting!

In Wonders

It has pitched a tent in the sky!
Its golden glow charms the
world in radiance;
Shining bright for all to see
God made the sun in wonders.

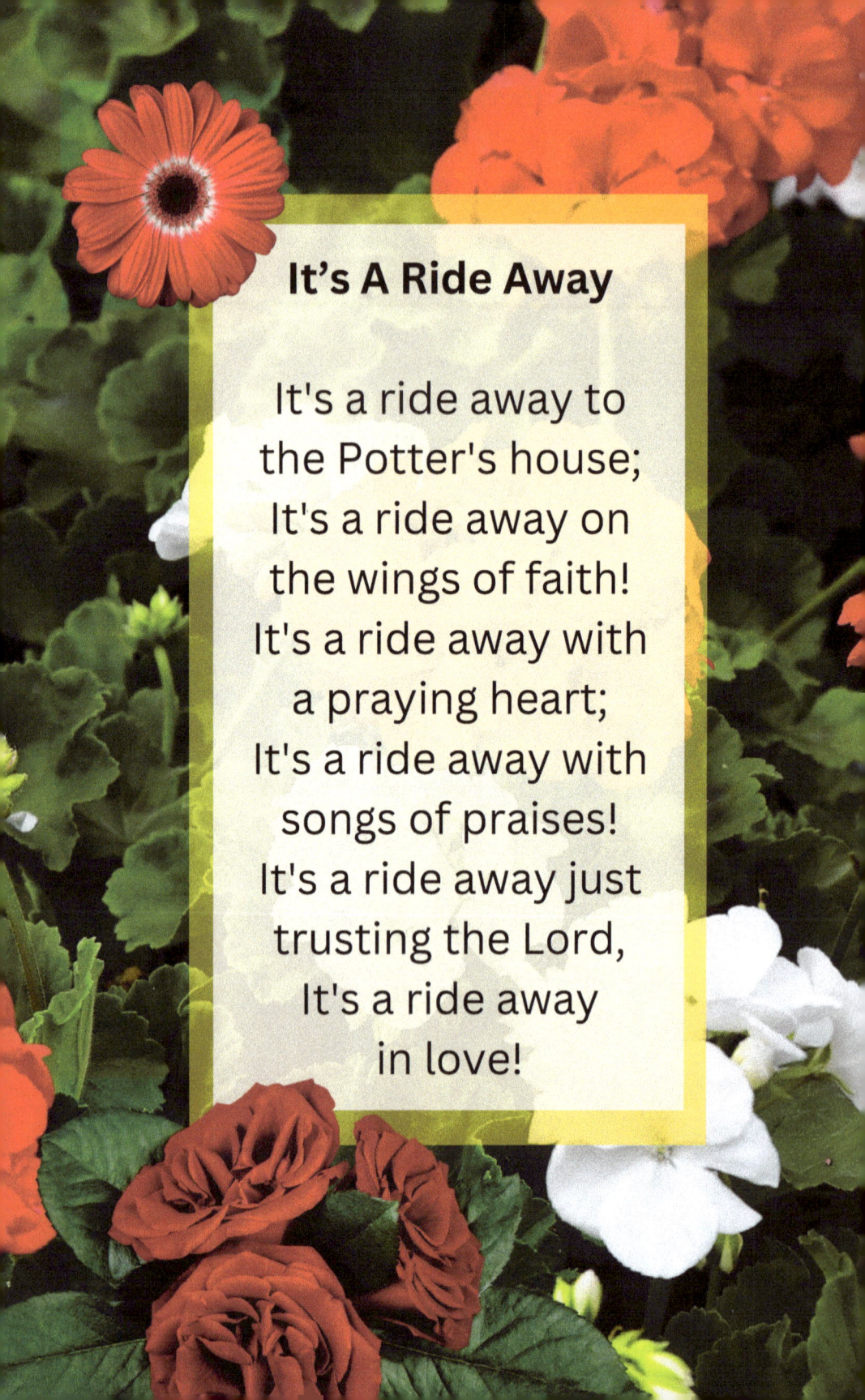

It's A Ride Away

It's a ride away to
the Potter's house;
It's a ride away on
the wings of faith!
It's a ride away with
a praying heart;
It's a ride away with
songs of praises!
It's a ride away just
trusting the Lord,
It's a ride away
in love!

It's Everything

It's everything lovely!
It's everything charming,
It's everything floral,
It's everything joyful!
Out in the month of May!

Jesus Knows

Jesus knows our
yesterday!
He understands our
today;
He is aware of our
tomorrow!
He knows our story
He can mend the
broken pieces;
Just trust in Him!

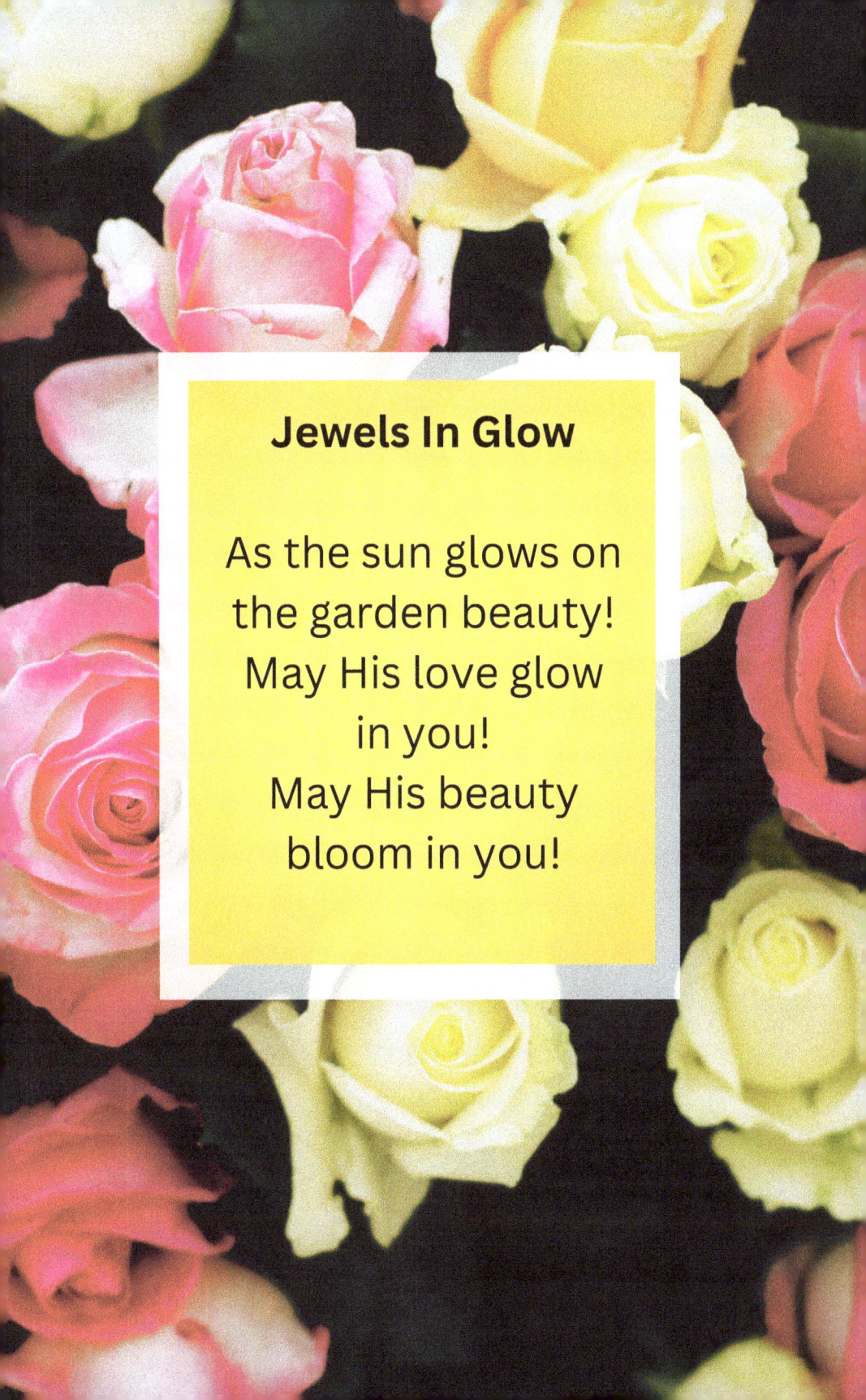

Jewels In Glow

As the sun glows on
the garden beauty!
May His love glow
in you!
May His beauty
bloom in you!

Jewels Of Joy

Blushing in bloomy radiance!
Sunkissed and rosey bright!
Beauty bubbles exuding joy,
She is an ornamental beauty,
A timeless treasure!

Joy Again

Pick up a rose
inhale its
fragrance
It is time for
joy again!

Give out a rose
Light up joy
It is time to
love again!

Joyful And Energizing

Love glows
subtly on
flowers,
with a
melodious
rhythm.

Joyful Blend

May love
blossom
your way
in sweet
whispers
of flowers.

Joyful Colours

Colours of Joy!
Colours of beauty,
Flashing love on a rosey
petally day!

Joyful Glow

Glowing in radiance,
gems of the garden;
filling the moments,
with joy!

Joyful Hug

When dawn kisses the sky!
May we hug the beauty of a new
day in love and joy!

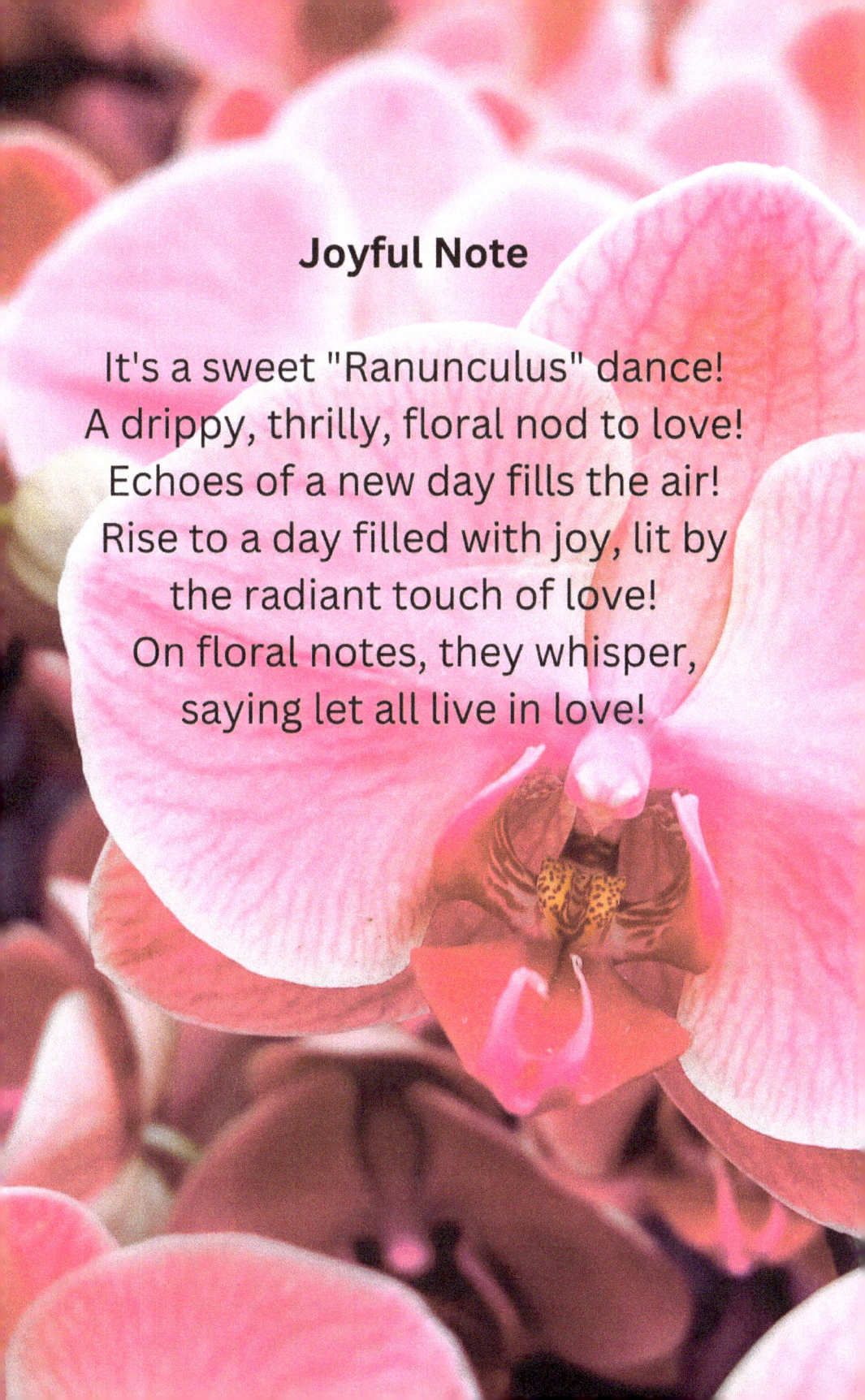

Joyful Note

It's a sweet "Ranunculus" dance!
A drippy, thrilly, floral nod to love!
Echoes of a new day fills the air!
Rise to a day filled with joy, lit by
the radiant touch of love!
On floral notes, they whisper,
saying let all live in love!

Laced In Love

It's a floral splash,
A love touch!
Laced in beauty,
Laced in love,
Laced in joy,
I glow in colours!

Let Your Home

Let your home
be lit by love;
Rays of joy
blooming
bright!

Let your home
be filled with
warmth;
Flowery cuddles,
Love to shine!

Let's Come Together

Inhale the goodness, of nature!
Take in His love!

Light Joy

Praise Him
who has made
all things
beautiful,
Beauty lights
the world in
joy!

Light The Day

Light the day
with joy!
May you be
favored by
the bountiful
blessings of
the day!

Light Up

Light the garden
with bountiful,
floral notes!
Let its fragrance,
wrap you in
bountiful floral,
bliss!

Live The Moment

Live the moment in love,
Chasing butterflies!
Picking up flowers!
Live the moment in joy!
Praising the Lord!
Exalting His name, Live in peace!

Living Hope

Jesus is my
living hope,
Jesus is all
to me,
Jesus is my
song!
my strength,
my peace,
Jesus is my
joy!

Love Bubbles

Aquamarine and Skystone,
crystals light the garden!
Like drizzles on the hilltop,
glistening and dewy;
A flash of love in the air!
Love bubbles in the air,
in crystals and joy.

Love Cascade

Be refreshed in the,
cascade of florals;
Take a dip in the,
essence of roses!

Love Expressed

It is love we sing!
It is love we wish,
It is love we hope,
It is love the,
stars sing about!
Love beautifies,
Love heals a hurting world;
It is love that,
unites us as one.

Love Glow

Glow in "Care!"
Shine in "Love!"
Light "Hope!"

Love Flame

Let love be a flame
in you, glowing with
luminescence.

Love Lace

Something sweetened by love!
Something spiced by love,
Something seasoned by love,
Something beautified by love,
Are whispers from the roses,
for you!

Love Lights

Love lights the fields
with beauty!
Glazes the flowers
with charm;
Envelops the world
in joy!

Love Plays

The petally drop of crystals,
The bloomy joy of roses!
Beautifying and energizing!
Love plays a fiddle.

Love Ride

Love sang me a sweet song,
on pearls of roses!
Love cuddled me in sweetly
scented petally wraps!
Love pinkly blooms my way!
Love gave me a ride, on the
feathery wings of love!

Love So Profound

It was love so profound
offered to me,
It was beauty, so real,
i saw!
Like daisies, bright and
beautiful;
It filled my heart, with
joy!
He dressed me,
in new garments!
He gave me,
a complete makeover;
He told me, i could;
"Walk with Him"
It was love so profound
offered to me;
It was Jesus!

Love Spring

Constantly
uplifted by
His, grace!

Constantly
renewed
by His,
mercies!

It's a joyful,
spring of love!

Love Tale

Sweet rosey knit!
Whispering rhythms
of love!
Kindling hopes-n-joy!
Bees cuddled in,
rosey pinky palettes!
Roses in twinkly glow!
A juicy love tale!

Love Unfolds

Love unfolds like a flower!
Everyday is a new experience!
Everyday is a new feel.

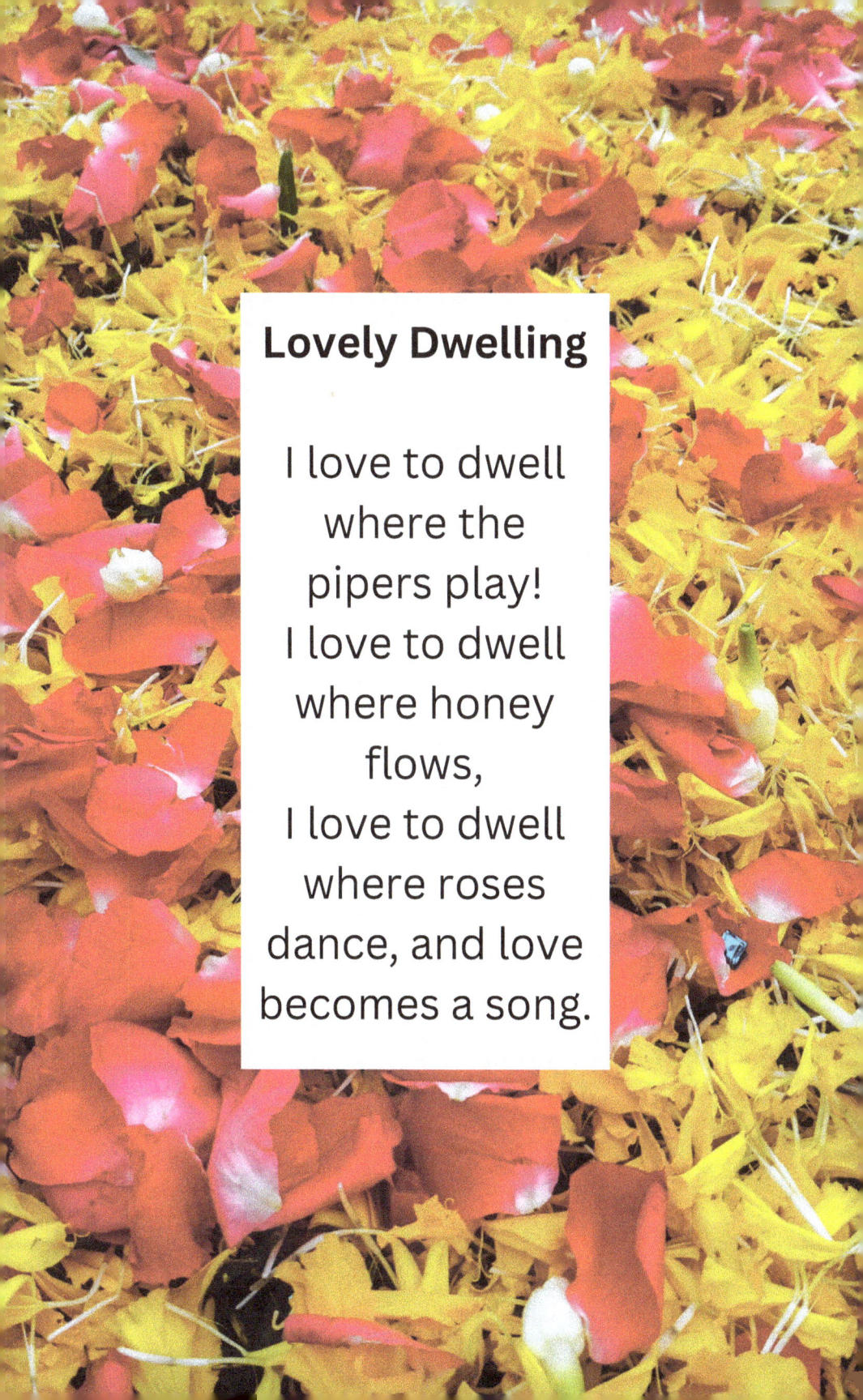

Lovely Dwelling

I love to dwell
where the
pipers play!
I love to dwell
where honey
flows,
I love to dwell
where roses
dance, and love
becomes a song.

Luminescence of Hope

In luminescence
of hope,
We spring forth
radiantly!
Flourishing,
in graceful
abundance,
We water the
garden in
floral drizzles,
of love!
We sing out
His praise!

Marbles In Bloom

Bubbles in glow!
Joy in florals!
Marbles in bloom,
Beauty-a-float!
Sparkles of the
season,
Colours of love,
glowing with joy;
Merry-Petally,
joy, a promise
of hope!

Merry Rhythms

Sweet fragrant
notes of love!
The awakening
of floral charm!
The joy of dewy,
blooms!
A toast to merry
dawn!
Love blooms in
flowers, with a
sweet-n-merry,
song!

More Than Roses

More than the scent of roses,
is the fragrance of His love!

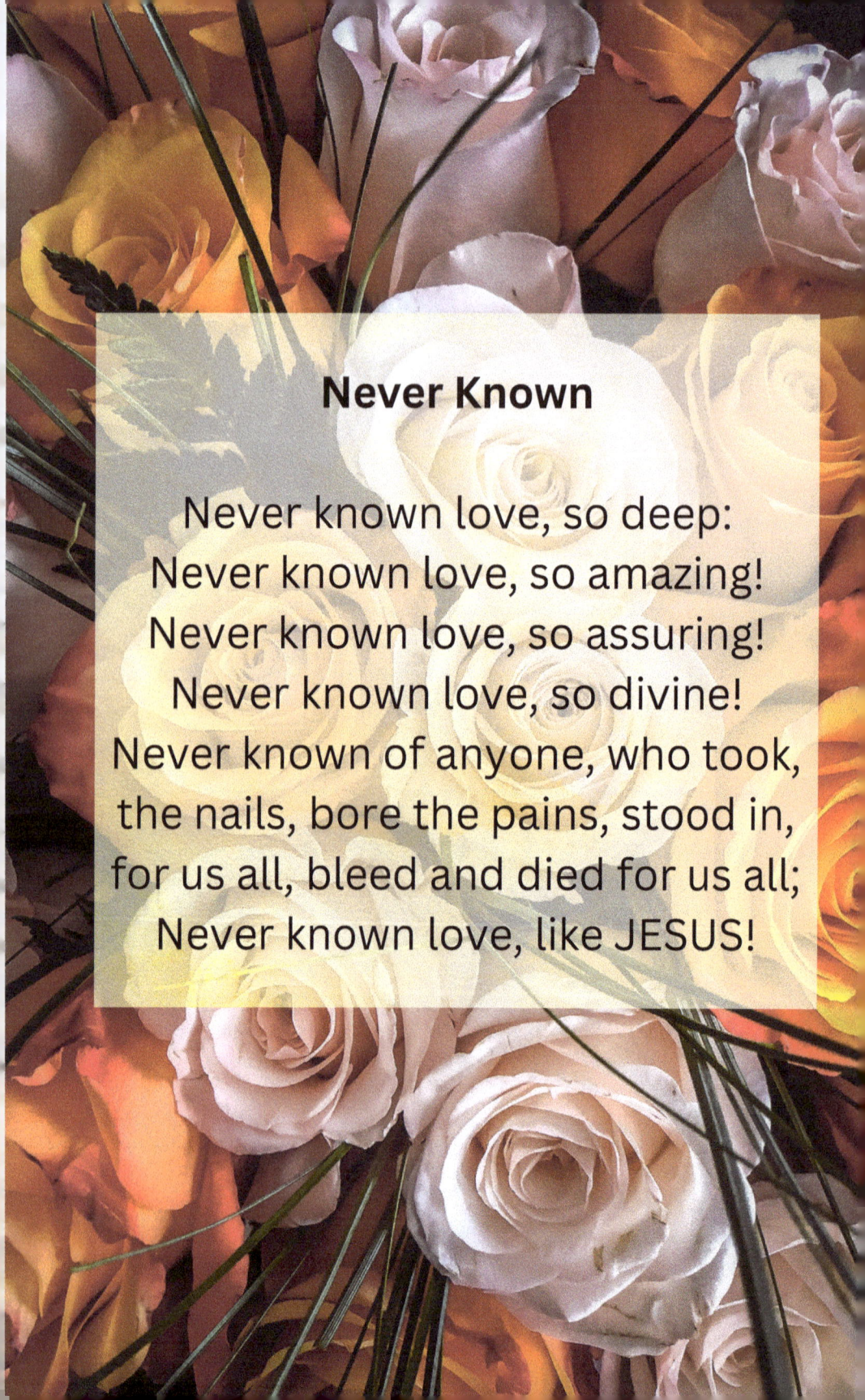

Never Known

Never known love, so deep:
Never known love, so amazing!
Never known love, so assuring!
Never known love, so divine!
Never known of anyone, who took,
the nails, bore the pains, stood in,
for us all, bleed and died for us all;
Never known love, like JESUS!

New Day Joy

In the joy of a new
day, may you be
filled with the
goodness of
the Lord;
In love, peace,
and strength,
may you,
prosper!

New Dawn

In sweet essence of the morning sun,
The glow of joy arrives!
New hopes arising with the rising sun!
In joyful rhythms of a new dawn,
Hearts are kindled with new songs of love,
New colours are seen from the rising horizon,
A new glow of hope!
In rays of beauty and love,
Nature sings a new tune!
In clusters of pearlescent glow,
I dance to a new dawn!

New Touch

Radiant-n-Joyful,
Precious-n-Regal,
It's a new touch
of favor,
A new glow of
grace!
A new wave of
joy!

A new feel of love!

Night Fantasy

How i see the moon, in all of its
glow, lighting up the night sky,
It's a time of renewed hope,
It's a time of favor!
It's a time to behold, the
wonders
of creation!
It's a time of joy!

Night Sky

I love to watch the night sky,
It tells of the power of God!
I love to gaze, at the sparkling
stars!
It tells of the wonders of God!
I love to watch, the glowing moon,
It tells of the love of God!
I love to watch the planets,
shine as gold in the sky!
It tells of the greatness of
God!
I love to watch the night sky,
It tells of the majesty of God!

Open Doors

"Prayer is the key, that
opens doors,
and lets the light in!"

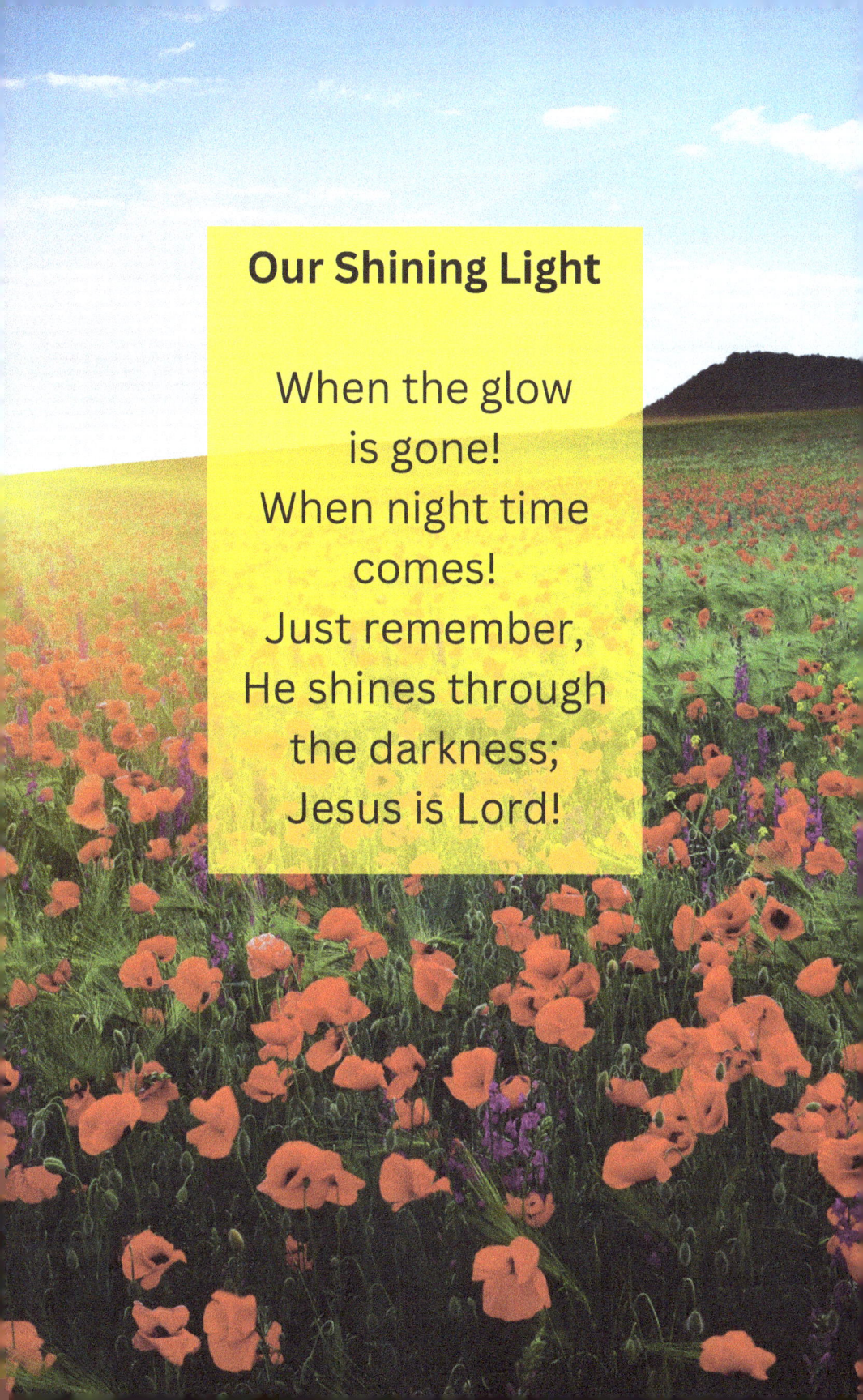

Our Shining Light

When the glow
is gone!
When night time
comes!
Just remember,
He shines through
the darkness;
Jesus is Lord!

Our Values

Our values of life
is what makes
the richness
of life;

Live life to the
fullest, in its
most beautiful,
and colourful,
pages.

Pearlescent Flower

Pearls-n-Glow!
Pearlescent
and sweetly,
adorning the
garden!
A floral bliss!

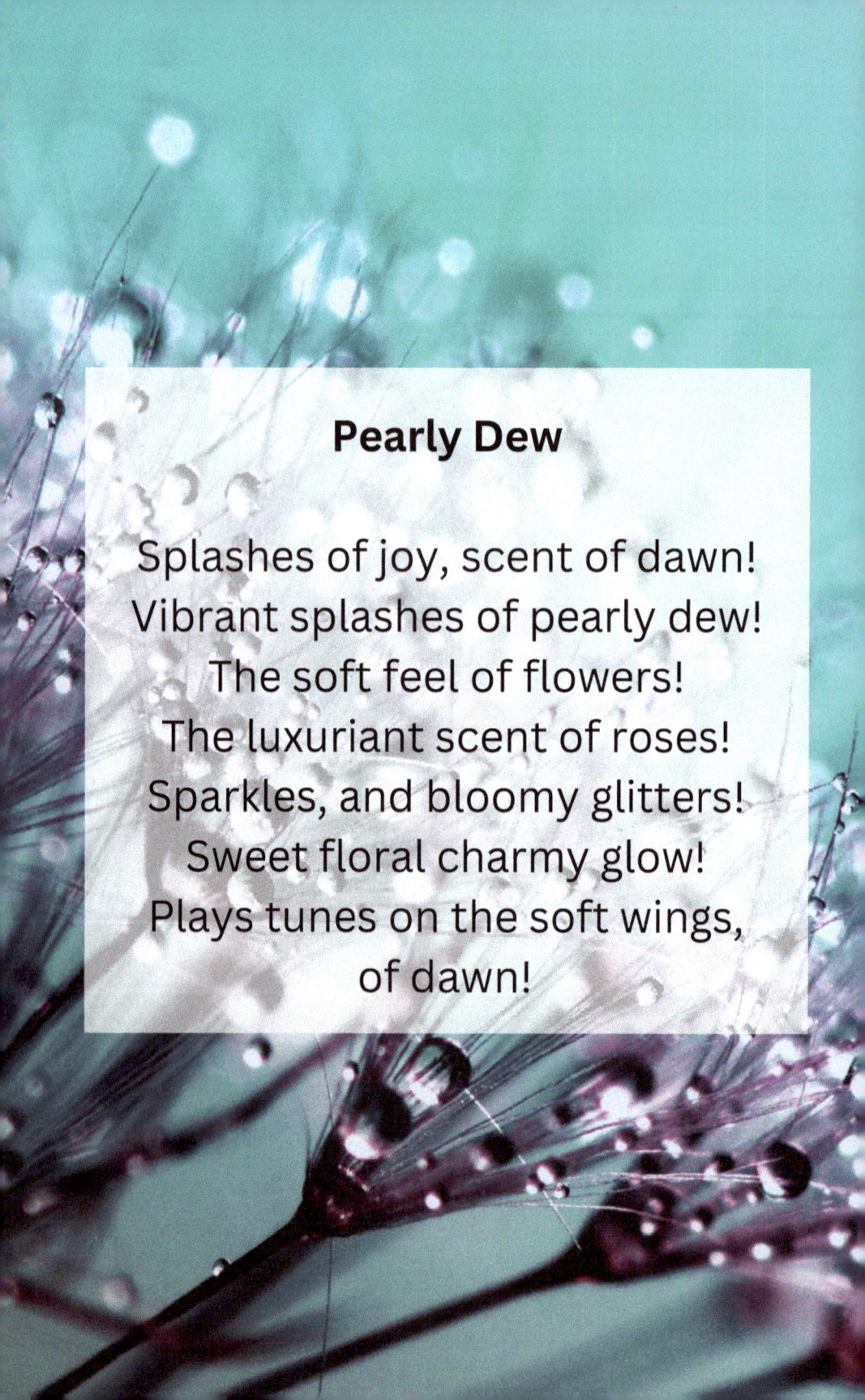

Pearly Dew

Splashes of joy, scent of dawn!
Vibrant splashes of pearly dew!
The soft feel of flowers!
The luxuriant scent of roses!
Sparkles, and bloomy glitters!
Sweet floral charmy glow!
Plays tunes on the soft wings,
of dawn!

Pearly Roses

A message lit with love,
from the pearly roses!
Love so divine!
Beauty so pinky sweet!
Curdles and bubbles!
Hugs and laughter!
It's our wish for you!

Pearly Sea

Pearls in drizzle,
Love-a-Float!
Joy glows like,
crystals on a
beautiful
pearly sea.

Petally Note

Play the
tunes of love,
on a petally
Note!

Sing the joy
of love, with
a rose bloom!

Petals In The Snow

Like a lady, in the garden, she smiles
at me;
Like a lady in waiting, she
glows in beauty!
Glowing in the snow, are
petals bright and beautiful.

Love glows wherever,
it finds a home;
Love illumines,
even the darkest
path.

Precious Bloom

Love blooms preciously,
in hearts of warmth,
and care, with a divine
touch of gold!

Precious Tunes

The joyful echoes of love!
Sweetly resounding in the air!
Love comes blushing in blooms:
With high notes of merry tunes!
Singing in Summer's blooms,
Precious tunes to calm the heart,
In sweet echoes, floral songs
resound!
Beauty is awakened on a thousand
fields!
Love is awakened in rhythms of
roses, Love lights the world with
joy!!
Roses touch the world with love!!

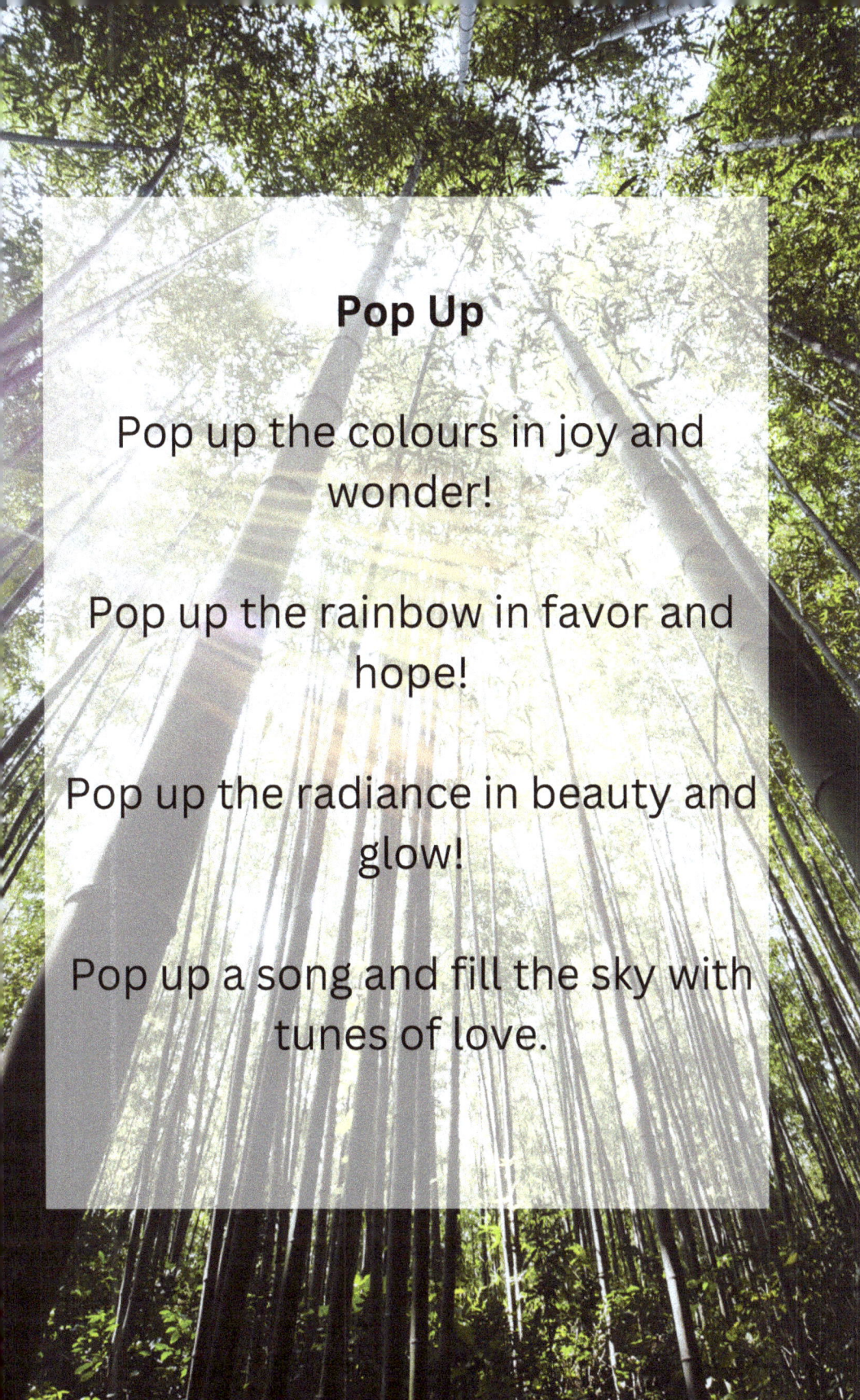

Pop Up

Pop up the colours in joy and wonder!

Pop up the rainbow in favor and hope!

Pop up the radiance in beauty and glow!

Pop up a song and fill the sky with tunes of love.

Pretty In Pink

She stands high,
pretty in pink!
Radiant in bloom,
adorned with,
pearls!
She speaks for,
the bold;
She sings for,
the weak;
A messenger, of
love!
A beauty, to
behold!
She is "ROSE!"

Purple Sapphire

Encrusted in crushed diamonds,
the precious "Purple Sapphire"
blooms among flowers!
It's a song among florals!
She is "Regal"
A sweet damsel!

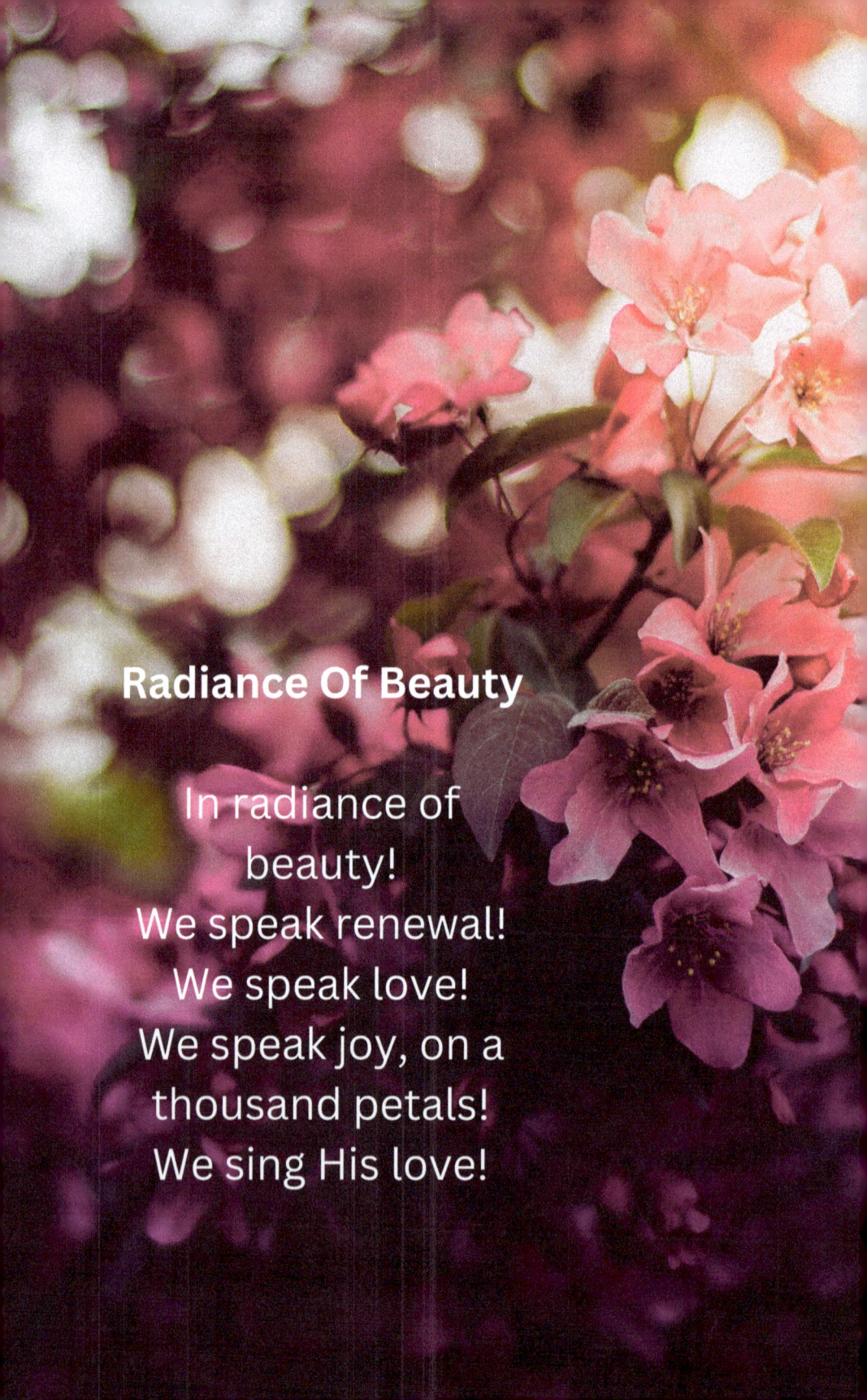

Radiance Of Beauty

In radiance of
beauty!
We speak renewal!
We speak love!
We speak joy, on a
thousand petals!
We sing His love!

Radiant Joy

In the abundance of
His mercies,
we flourish
beautifully!
In the glow of His
grace,
we bloom radiantly!
In the radiance of
His love,
we glorify His name!

Rhythms Of Hope

The flowers, spring forth, elegant
in bloom, vibrant and joyful!
Lush in beauty, colorful, and bright,
There is a spark of joy!
Songs can be heard, in a land that,
was desolate;
There is rekindling of hope!!

Rhythms Of Kindness

Kindness is like a tree,
lit with lush blossoms,
You sow seeds, of
kindness, they are
touched and watered!
The fragrance, of your
kindness, brings notes,
of joy, love, and hope,
It paints the world, in
radiant colours;
The kindness, you
show, flowers by
your side!
Bloom in kindness,
always!

Rise Pearls

Pearls of the garden,
Joy of the seasons,
It's a beauty find,
whenever you arise!

Roses-n-Glow

Twinkles and Sparkles,
Roses-n-Glitters!
Rose Quartz in bloom!
Pink Topaz in glow,
Joy! Oh Joy! it's all,
Joy in "Bloomy Land."

Rosette Street

It's a beautiful
place to be at,
"Rosette Street,"
It's a beautiful
place to watch
the glow!
It's beautiful at,
"Rosette Street,"
when the sun,
hugs the roses,
in love.

Rosey Wrap

It's a cocktail of love,
A joyful blend of flowers!
Freshen your day with,
sweet notes;
Let the scent of roses,
give you a wrap!

Saturate Me

Saturate me with,
Your goodness,
O Lord!

Let Your,
blessings come,
as dew over me!

Scented Bloom

Love is a scented
bloom, that
springs forth joy,
with uplifting,
and rejuvenating,
Notes.

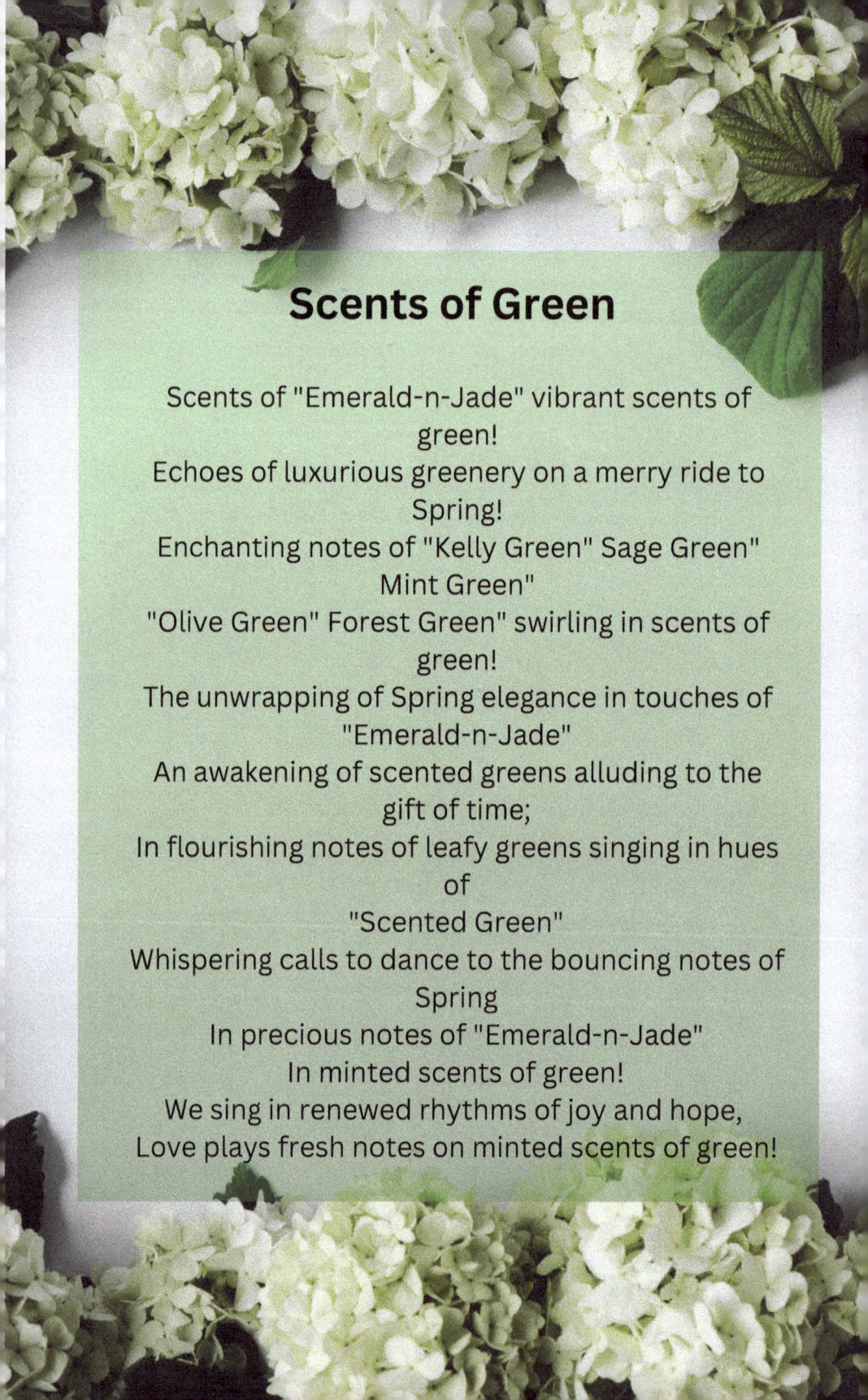

Scents of Green

Scents of "Emerald-n-Jade" vibrant scents of green!
Echoes of luxurious greenery on a merry ride to Spring!
Enchanting notes of "Kelly Green" Sage Green" Mint Green"
"Olive Green" Forest Green" swirling in scents of green!
The unwrapping of Spring elegance in touches of "Emerald-n-Jade"
An awakening of scented greens alluding to the gift of time;
In flourishing notes of leafy greens singing in hues of
"Scented Green"
Whispering calls to dance to the bouncing notes of Spring
In precious notes of "Emerald-n-Jade"
In minted scents of green!
We sing in renewed rhythms of joy and hope,
Love plays fresh notes on minted scents of green!

Sweet Cuddles

Fresh notes of roses, lit in scented
adoration!
Playing in the soft brushes of the
billowy wind!
Touches of scented charm, sweet, and
soft!
A whimsical wrap of flowery cuddles!
Singing from precious blooms in
joyful rhythms, Melodious voices ring
out in sweet accord!
Love notes play out from the heart of
roses in breezy tunes
Oh sweet rose, your voice is heard in
your
"Scent Of Charm"
Your love is felt in your petals!
You light my world with joy!
You are a delight to me!

Shawls Of Favor

May the aura
of favor be
wrapped around
you always!

Shine Brightly

In the glow of,
His love!
May you shine,
brightly everyday.

Shine Forth

Shine forth!
and sing, His praise

Touch the rainbow!
Touch the
sky!

Touch the world with
vibrant colours;
Touch the stars!

Shores Of Joy

May beauty,
reawake you
to a new
beginning!
On the shores
of joy, may you
always dwell.

Sing His Praise

There is none like You,
On a sweet and joyful note,
we sing out Your praise;

"O Lord You Reign!"

Sing Oh Sing

Let it sing your
name!
Let it tell of your
love!
As the flowers
bloom!
O Lord,
your name is
exalted!

Sing On

Sing on!
Dance on!
It's time to
celebrate,
the
wonders,
of His,
"LOVE."

Song Of A Tree

I am a tall tree, blessed to be one!
I am decorated with ornaments, of
white dainty blossoms in Spring;
I am decorated with ornaments of
red orangy berries, in Summer!
The Fall season, keeps me dressed
in leaves with exotic hues of red,
yellow, orange, and brown!
The Winter season, leaves me coated,
with soft white pearly snow!
I am glad to be made a tree!

Song Of Joy

Sing a new
song of joy!
Sing a new
note of His,
love!
Sing a new
touch of His,
presence.

Songs Of Renewal

Songs of,
"Renewal"
Songs of,
"Joy"
May you,
be
"Refreshed"
in
His,
"Love."

Sparkles Of Joy

It's a sparkle of joy!
Fluorescence of hope,
sails through the sky!
There is a sizzling
beauty, that awakes
the morning sky!
Brightness is lit upon,
the earth!
Echoes of dawn plays
like a flute!
Hope is reborn!

Sparkly Beauty

Sparkling notes of Summer,
leaves a lingering feeling of delight!
Beauty lights the air!
Hope blooms in beauty.

Sparkly Wonder

Sparkles-n-Sprinkles! Night time in twinkles!
Diamonds in starry drizzles all across the sky!
Drizzles-n-dazzles in the beautiful wonder of a
love-lit starry night!
It's all sprinkly wonder!
It's all sparkly-n-glowy joy!
It's all twinkly radiance coming down in
sparkles, It's all drizzly-n-dazzling when the
night sky dances to
the rhythm of the glittery stars!
It's all drippy dazzles when the stars play the
flute
at night,
Drippy-n-Dazzling! it's a night time wonder of
dancing,
"Stars!"

Spice Of Favor

A taste of love!
A flavour of joy!
A tang of beauty!
A spice of favor!
Adds zest to life.

Spring Beauty

I love the scent of Spring!
I love the joy it gives!
I love the notes of Spring!
I love the hope it brings!
I love the blooms of Spring!
I love the beauty they bring!

Spring Forth

May joy spring forth as fresh blooms,
in your home everyday!

Sweet And Sensual

Warm and Vibrant,
are the notes of,
Summer!
Sweet and Sensual,
are the notes of,
the Rose!
Sweet bells of,
florals!
An epitome of,
beauty!

Sweet and Exquisite

Sweet and exquisite garden, lit in the
chorus of roses!
Sweet and exquisite, a warm touch of love!
Sweet scents of love finds a home in the
nest of roses, Sweet touch of love flows
from the heart of roses!
Sweet whispery notes of love plays on
lacey petals!
A charming bloom! A dainty precious floral
ruby!
Sweet and exquisite is the garden that
holds the rose gems, Sweet and exquisite
are the beauty blooms that spice up
the garden in alluring wonder!

Sweet August Bells

Sweet August bells!
Dainties of Summer!
Sweet chimes of Opals!
Awake to Summer joy!

Sweet Assurance

More than the
bouquet of roses,
is the sweetness,
and comfort, of
His, "Great Love!"

Sweet Delight

In a garden of
sweet delight,
In a garden of
blooming,
"Emeralds,"
In a garden,
tucked with,
sweet spices!
Springs forth
a damsel of,
pure delight.

Sweet Essence

Beauty in Spring,
Radiance in Summer!
Golden glowy in Fall,
Glittery in Winter!
The petals go singing!

Sweet Harmony

In radiance, and
love!
In warmth, and
beauty;
Kissed by the,
sun!
Touched by love!
I glow in colours.

Sweet Joy

May your pathway, be
beautified with
the notes of flourishing
blooms!

Sweet Love Expression

Twinkles in
glowy pink!
A sweet spin
of blooms!
A sultry love
expression!
Drizzling in
floral beauty!

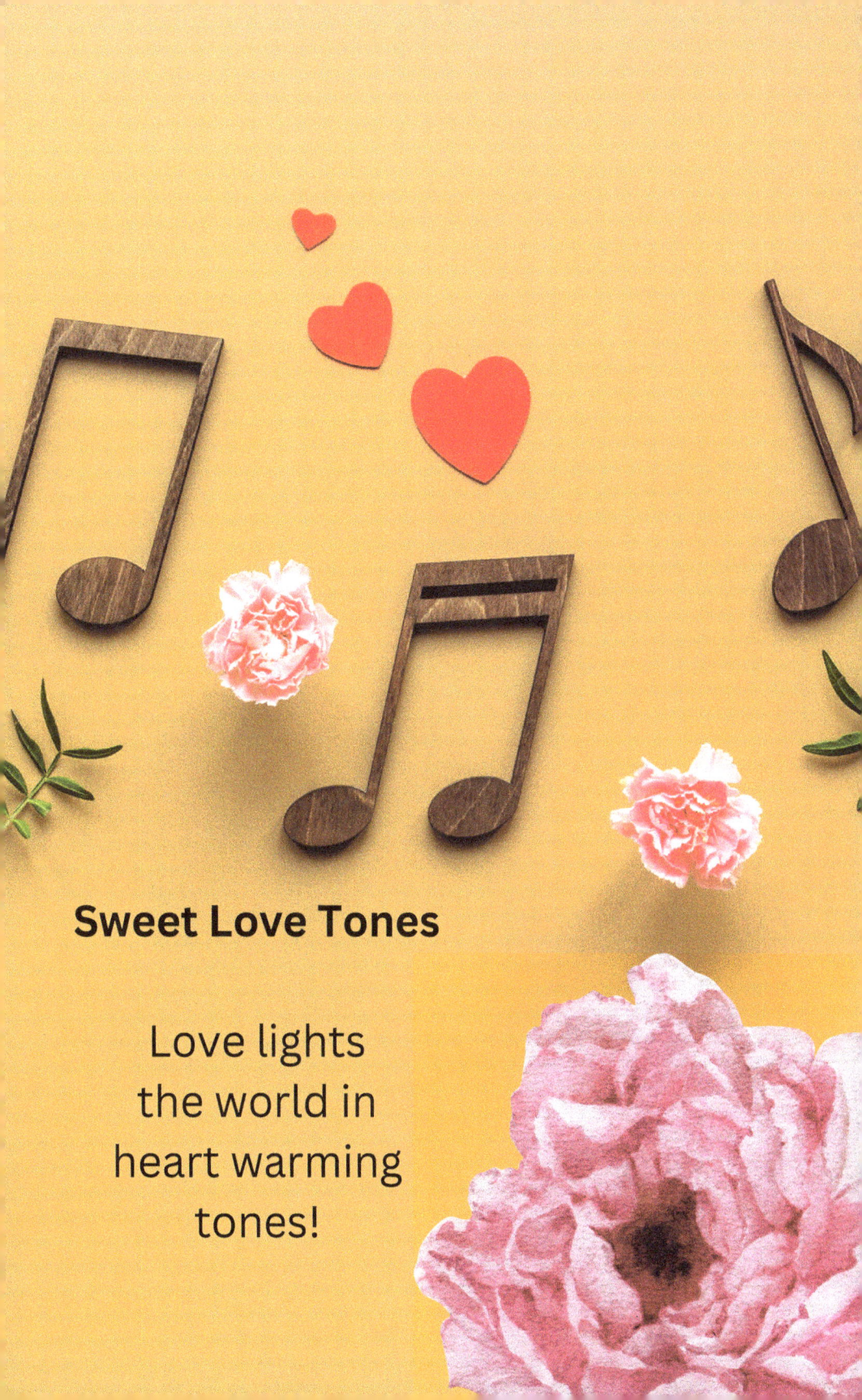

Sweet Love Tones

Love lights the world in heart warming tones!

Sweet Ruby Rose

Sweet and Sensual, Rosey and Divine!
Blooming in ruby splendor
A rose for a gem! A rosey treasure!
In cuddles of petally radiance, She glows
sweetly in love!
A rose for a Princess, A rose for a Damsel,
She stands precious with scents of love!
A warmth of glow! A bloom of delight!!
She touches hearts with joy!
She warms my hands with love!
She is my love! She is my Rose!
She is my ruby in bloomy splendor!

Sweet Spice

Let the colours of delight, be your portion,
Let the colours of warmth, invigorate you!
Let the colours of hope, strengthen you!

Swing In

The glow of love,
shines brightly!
Let love blossom!
Let love shine!
Let love swing,
sweetly your way!

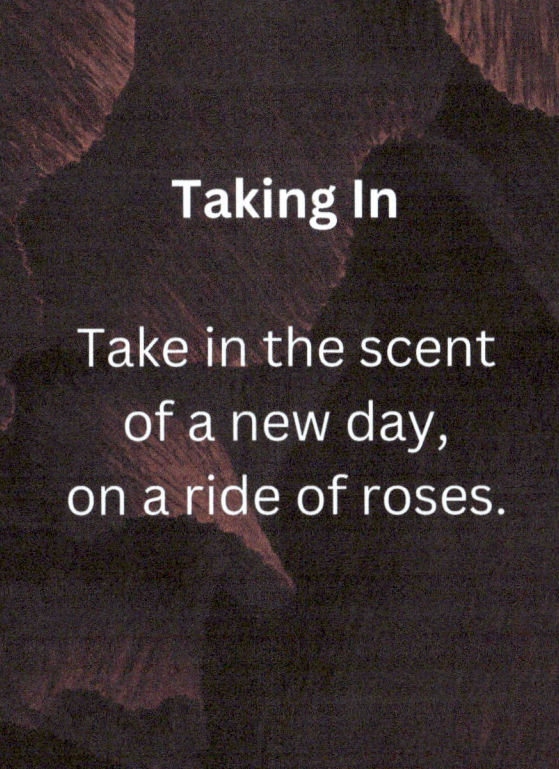

Taking In

Take in the scent
of a new day,
on a ride of roses.

Tell you

If i could tell you, i will,
tell you of love!
If i could sing to you,
i will sing to you of,
peace; cheery notes,
to gladden the heart!
What the world needs,
is love, joy, peace,
hugs, and laughter!
What the world needs,
is JESUS!

The Fields

When the Spring fields blossoms,
Let me sing your favour!
When the Summer fields flourish,
Let me sing your love,
When the Fall fields heap the foliage,
Let me sing your joy!
When the Winter fields slumber,
Let me sing your peace.

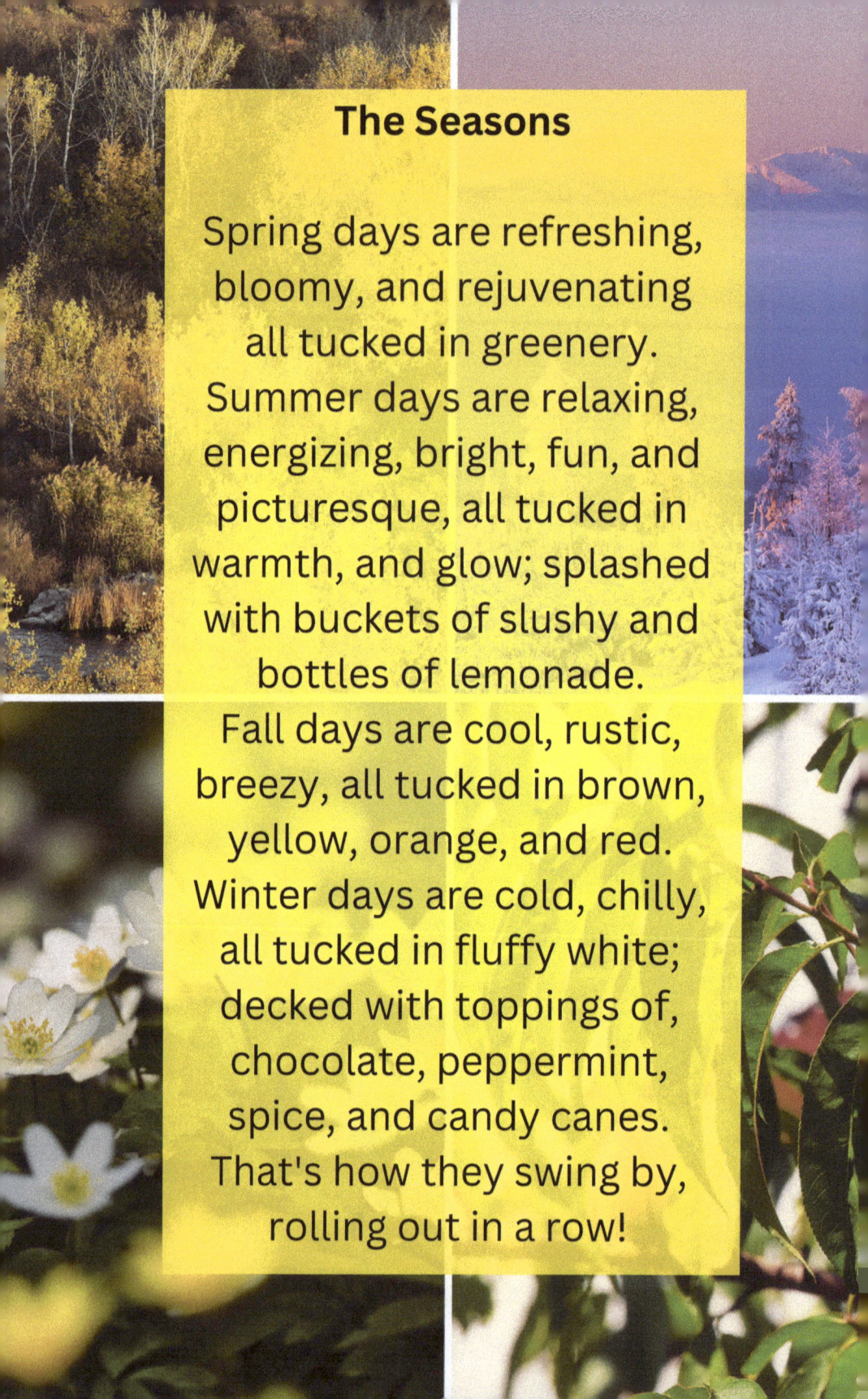

The Seasons

Spring days are refreshing,
bloomy, and rejuvenating
all tucked in greenery.
Summer days are relaxing,
energizing, bright, fun, and
picturesque, all tucked in
warmth, and glow; splashed
with buckets of slushy and
bottles of lemonade.
Fall days are cool, rustic,
breezy, all tucked in brown,
yellow, orange, and red.
Winter days are cold, chilly,
all tucked in fluffy white;
decked with toppings of,
chocolate, peppermint,
spice, and candy canes.
That's how they swing by,
rolling out in a row!

Tonic Of Love

Love is like
a tonic,
energizing,
and
refreshing;
with sweet
accords to
warm the,
heart.

Torch Of Love

May the brightness,
of His love, be as
a torch along your
way;

May you always,
know the fullness,
of His love.

Treasures Of Joy

Like golden treasures,
lost and found, she sits
on my hand in beauty,
and warmth.

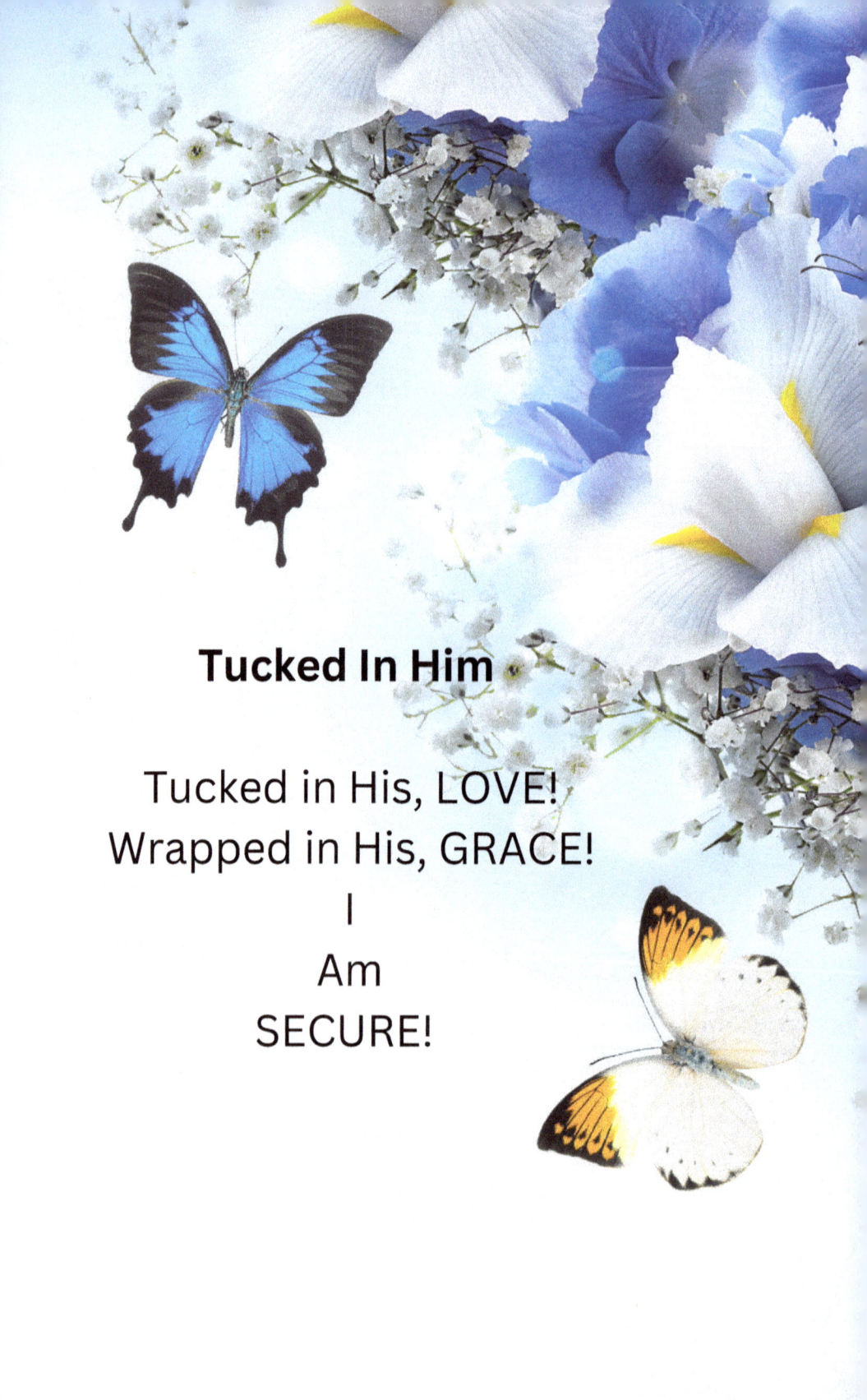

Tucked In Him

Tucked in His, LOVE!
Wrapped in His, GRACE!
I
Am
SECURE!

Tune Of Hope

Joy awakes the dawn, with a new
tune of hope, it's time to sing again!

Tunes Of Love

Love blooms
in many islands,
Glows in many
hearts!

Love glows on flowers!
Silently they speak!
Greatly they care.

Unchanging Love

When seasons change,
When rhythms change!
He remains the same!
His grace is forever,
His love is forever!
His peace is forever!

Veil Of Hope

A veil of colour, a run of rays,
A lush of beauty, a ray of hope!
A touch of glow and love, the
dancing rays of joy!
The opalescent glow of charm...
The enchanting notes of beauty...
Fascinated by the tones of love
on the spreading wings of flowers.
The white-throated sparrow sings
in sweet tunes;
"Oh-sweet-Canada-Canada"
Enamored with the musical notes
of sparrows, hope comes anew in
twinkling radiance; There is a veil
of hope in the enchanting tones of
beauty.

Vibrant And Colourful

Vibrant and Dewy!
Regal and Colourful,
Jewels so sumptuous,
and delectable in bloom!
Jewels of love and glow,
A beauty bloom in radiance.

Vibrant Notes

Frilly-n-Lacey!
Sweet-n-Vibrant!
Nutty-n-Graceful!
Are the rhythms,
of Spring!

Watch Us

Watch us sing,
Summer!
Watch us dance,
Summer!
Watch us play,
the tunes,
of Summer!
on a sweet,
love note.

Whispers of Dawn

In colourful whispers of
glowy dawn, May Your love
shine graciously on us!
May the scent of a new day
bring joy our way!
May the radiance of Your
grace, be upon us!
May the sparkly glow of
dawn bring beauty our way!
May we know the fullness
of Your love, O Lord!

Whispering Love

Whisper me your,
love, on sweet
petals!
Whisper me your,
care, on the ride
of floral scents;
Whisper me your,
wishes, on the
tones of golden
floral notes.

Wishing You Happiness

Wishing you happiness,
on a warm sunny day!
Wishing you happiness,
on a beautiful starry,
night!
Wishing you happiness,
upon a thousand
strings!
Wishing you, the glow,
and the radiance, of
happiness!
Wishing you happiness,
always!

Your Charm

A rose is a beauty,
it stands by its name!
A daisy is a gem bloom,
it sings love and renewal;
A star shines, it plays its
game, in dazzling beauty
it lights the night sky!
He has placed something,
in you, a gemstone, so
let it shine!
Be who you are designed,
to be;
Glow in your own charm.

Your Majesty

Your majesty is sang in the clouds,
Your power is echoed in the wind!
Your love is chanted in the heavens!
There is none like You, O Lord.

www.ingramcontent.com/pod-product-compliance
Lightning Source LLC
Chambersburg PA
CBHW041626140626
46547CB00030B/1055